Busy Beavers

by Dale Lundberg

Harcourt
SCHOOL PUBLISHERS

Cover, ©Tom and Pat Leeson; p.3, ©Tom McHugh/Photo Researchers, Inc.; p.4, ©W. Perry Conway/CORBIS; p.5, ©Taylor S. Kennedy/National Geographic Image Collection; p.6, ©Michio Hoshino/Minden Pictures; p.7, ©Konrad Wothe/Minden Pictures; p.8, ©Steve Greer/AlaskaPhotoGraphics; p.9, ©Momatiuk–Eastcott/Corbis; p.10, ©Jack Wilburn/Animals Animals; p.11, ©TIM FITZHARRIS/Minden Pictures; p.12, ©Dominique Braud/Animals Animals; p.13, ©W. Perry Conway/CORBIS; p.14, ©Erwin and Peggy Bauer/Animals Animals.

Printed in China

ISBN 10: 0-15-350694-6
ISBN 13: 978-0-15-350694-9

Ordering Options
ISBN 10: 0-15-350600-8 (Grade 3 On-Level Collection)
ISBN 13: 978-0-15-350600-0 (Grade 3 On-Level Collection)
ISBN 10: 0-15-357911-0 (package of 5)
ISBN 13: 978-0-15-357911-0 (package of 5)

4 5 6 7 8 9 10 0940 12 11 10 09

Have you ever heard the saying "as busy as a beaver"? Well, beavers are extremely busy animals. They are best known for building dams. A dam is a wall of branches built across a stream.

Beavers are rodents, small mammals that have teeth for gnawing. Beavers may grow to be 4 feet (1.22 m) long, including their flat, pancake-shaped tails. They are also quite heavy. Beavers may weigh up to 75 pounds (34 kg).

Beavers live along the banks of rivers and streams. There they build their homes. Parts of their homes are under the water. Beaver homes are called lodges. About eight beavers live in one lodge. Lodges are made of sticks, twigs, logs, and mud.

A beaver's lodge has different sections that are called dens. There is a den for feeding and a den for sleeping. All of the dens are above the water so that the beavers stay dry. Most lodges have two openings that lead to the water.

Beavers also build dams. Dams block the flow of water in a stream. The water on one side of the stream gets deeper. The beavers build their lodges in the deeper water because the deep water is less likely to freeze. This way beavers can get to their lodges from under the water even in the wintertime.

The beavers line their dams with twigs, leaves, and rocks. The dam is strong enough to slow down the flow of water in a fast-moving stream.

Dams can also be very big. In fact, beavers have built dams that are hundreds of feet long. So how does a beaver build such a large structure? That's easy—with its teeth and flat tail.

Beavers are good builders because of their strong body parts. The first thing you might notice about a beaver is its large teeth. The beaver has four front teeth, two on the top and two on the bottom. They are very sharp at the edges.

These teeth make it easy for the beaver to chew down trees and branches. A beaver's teeth continue to grow throughout its life! They stay the same length because the beaver wears them down by chewing.

Beavers use their tails to help them swim. The tails guide them through the water. Their hind paws are large and webbed, which also helps them swim. Their front paws are like little hands. Beavers dig mud, hold branches, and even comb their fur with their front paws!

Beavers are very social animals. Young beavers stay with their parents until they are about two years old.

To build a dam, beavers must first cut down trees. The beavers hug the trees with their paws, and then they begin to chew. The beaver tilts its head to one side and takes a bite.

The beavers chomp away. Bite by bite, wood chips fall from the tree, and soon the tree falls down. Next, the beavers chew the branches off the tree.

In the stream, beavers lay down sticks and rocks. This will make up the bottom of the dam. Beavers are very strong. They use their paws and bodies to push the trees into the stream. The trees stick into the mud at the bottom of the stream. The tangle of tree branches reels in the rushing water, so the water in the stream begins to slow down.

The beavers build the dam higher and higher. They wind thin strands of wood and leaves among the larger branches, and they pack the dam with stones and mud. Soon the dam reaches across the stream.

Sometimes beavers chew down trees far away from a dam. To get the trees to the dam, the beavers dig shallow canals, or long ditches, that fill with water from the stream. The beavers push the trees into the canals, and then the trees float down to the dam.

Two busy beavers can build a 10-foot (3 m) dam in just a few days! The water on one side of the dam is deep. The deep water protects the beavers from animals that prey on them. Beavers can escape by diving into the deep water.

When fall arrives, beavers store food for winter near their lodges. They will need to spend a lot of time in their lodges to keep warm and safe.

The beavers begin building a lodge by placing
sticks, logs, and stones on the bottom of the stream.
Next, the beavers begin to carve out little rooms,
or dens. They dive underwater. Using their strong
teeth, they chew and chomp away. A beaver can hold
its breath underwater for fifteen minutes! Then the
beavers spiral up, cutting into the center of the lodge.
The beavers work inside the lodge until they are above
the water level, and then they create their dens.

After a swim, the beavers dry themselves off in the lower den. They also eat their meals there. Beavers sleep in the upper den. Beavers make their beds out of grass and bits of wood.

To keep the cold out of the lodge, beavers pack the outside with mud. One opening is left at the top of the lodge so that air can get inside. In the winter, the mud freezes. This keeps the air inside the lodge warm.

In winter, the beavers are warm in their lodge. They leave the lodge through the underwater openings to gather their favorite foods, such as tree bark. Then they return to the lodge to eat. Each day, the beavers fix any holes in their dams.

During the winter, young beavers are born. They are called kits. When springtime comes, the young beavers come out to play.

For the older beavers, spring means it is time to build again. They stay busy all year.

Think Critically

1. What is the first thing a beaver must do when building a dam?

2. Why do beavers have such sharp teeth?

3. What do you think happens to the water in a stream once beavers build their dam there?

4. What might happen to the beavers' lodge if the water in the stream dried up?

5. What did you like most about this book?

 Science

Design a Dam Look at the pictures and think about how a beaver builds its dam. Then think about how you would build a dam. Draw a diagram of your dam.

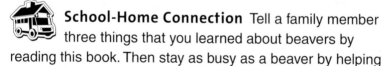 **School-Home Connection** Tell a family member three things that you learned about beavers by reading this book. Then stay as busy as a beaver by helping out at home.

Word Count: 966